CONDITIONAL DESIGN
An Introduction to Elemental Architecture

Di Mari, Anthony

Conditional Design: An Introduction to Elemental Architecture

BIS Publishers
Borneostraat 80-A
1094 CP Amsterdam
The Netherlands
T +31 (0)20 5150230
bis@bispublishers.com
www.bispublishers.com

ISBN: 978-90-6369-365-7
9th printing 2023

CONDITIONAL DESIGN
An Introduction to Elemental Architecture

Anthony Di Mari

BISPUBLISHERS

Foreword

Since publishing *Operative Design: A Catalogue of Spatial Verbs*, Anthony and I have had the opportunity to test ideas from the book hands on, working with design students through various studios and workshops. In employing the concepts from *Operative Design* as a pedagogical approach, we saw a natural progression toward creating a framework that could highlight the various conditions that were being created through the volumetric operations. As students' work became more sophisticated and complex, moving beyond the abstract volumetric studies, a new catalogue of these conditions/opportunities began to emerge. These ideas show how one could continue using the logic developed in *Operative Design* in order to further develop an architectural proposal.

The conditions shown in this book are also a set of iterations and design possibilities, set to instigate further study and exploration. They are directly tied to the original volumetric manipulations, but push it one step further -- seeing what those original operative verbs can yield, within an existing spatial condition, and what new conditions they themselves could create, through the addition of an aspect we deliberately kept abstract in the first book: the factor of scale.

Conditional Design translates scale through three basic architectural elements: vertical circulation, apertures, and site. These three elements are each fundamental to architecture in that they inherently connect constructed space back to the individual experiencing it. In essence, all three are about connection - connection within spaces, connection from within a space to without, and connection between a space and its surrounding site. I see *Conditional Design* as a natural continuation to the discussion started by *Operative Design* in that it proposes a bridge between abstract volumetric operations and what those operations could yield, through responding to programmatic requirements and given site conditions within a consistent methodology.

It should be noted that this is but one follow-up continuation to the large, abstracted base we began to construct in *Operative Design*. The fundamental basis of *Conditional Design* is its proposed use as a tool; it is meant to be an approach, not definitive or defined, that can be applied iteratively for various uses, conditions, and needs.

For those learning about spatial design, it emphasizes the deliberation inherent in how a designer makes design moves, and what those moves yield: it connects the design process with the character of the space created. As a designer, this is what I find most exciting about this book -- that it continues to delineate the various paths we can use as we approach a given project, beginning from abstract spatial play, to balancing program and site, in order to create truly intriguing, complex, and inspiring spaces.

Nora Yoo
June 2014

Introduction

This book is a natural sequential project to *Operative Design: A Catalogue of Spatial Verbs*. In *Operative Design*, spatial formation was construed as a process that could be derived from fundamental actions, and the book indexed a lexicon of illustrated verbs to activate architectural inquiry and to ignite the design process. This book builds squarely upon that base.

Spatially, the conditional is the result of the operative. As one manipulates volumes with operative verbs, different spatial conditions start to emerge. At that moment of volumetric manipulation, the designer is presented with an opportunity to consider one of several conditional opportunities: to connect one volume to another volume, to open the volume to receive light or entry, and to situate the volumes in relation to a ground plane, or consider how the set of manipulated volumes relate to and affect the ground condition.

For example, when two volumes are arranged to **overlap** with each other, one volume rests atop the other, and there is an interior zone that both volumes share as a result of the operation. Within that zone, one can establish the connection between both volumes. The operation has yielded both a formal strategy and revealed the connection between the volumes; simultaneously, the spatial moment defined by the operation allows the designer to consider the internal qualities of the design move they have just created. When one **carves** away at a volume, the act of removing a part of the volume allows the designer to question and at the same time confirm that this move sets up another spatial opportunity, to create apertures in the area of the subtraction, for example.

This systematic approach minimizes random placement of these elements and integrates them with a design method. One should still be critical of such methodical moves, because design should still be responsive to conditions outside of volumetric operations, including program, light, and access. These manipulations might react to an already existing condition or create a new set of conditions based on the operation and the ground plane. As a method, conditional design is a bridge between abstract volumetric manipulations and design that considers program, site, scale, and structure.

Elemental Architecture : Code + Character

By setting up a systematic process, opportunities for a focused design are facilitated by a set of deliberate moves. This can be referred to as a code of design and an attempt to develop a design methodology. In using the word code, the key goal is not a clear legibility of form, but a clear legibility of process. The design logic that results from the systematic approach creates consistency in the process and, ideally, the result. This does not suggest anything short of multiple iterations, for the system contains a variety of design conditions based on the original operations. It is a system of options. As in *Operative Design*, *Conditional Design* is in search of variation through a directed working method, which in turn can be used as a basis upon which to critique the design.

Ultimately, the end design relates back to the actual spaces that are created, and how one would experience the volumetric manipulations. The conditional moves allow for the incorporation of elements such as light, ground, and circulation, while acknowledging and addressing the experience of these spaces in the context of existing conditions and constraints of a design project.

Revisiting Planes: Connection + Aperture + Ground

Conditional Design takes the original volumes from *Operative Design* and considers them as planar constructs. In this sense, *Conditional Design* will stray from its spatially abstract predecessor. *Operative Design* presented opportunities to iteratively study volumetric relationships. In order to further understand these volumetric studies, it is imperative to give the volumetric envelope a scale. The operations still stand as isolated moments initially, and eventually build upon themselves through combinations and aggregations, with the focus now on the planes comprising the volumes as they start to craft spatial character. The type of operation (single, multiple, add, displace, or subtract), again helps to index how these various conditions are created, while highlighting the iterative operative process. With this focus now on the volume planes, the interior of the volumes is considered, as well as the resultant interior/exterior dynamic.

The reading of planes extends to that of the ground plane. As *Conditional Design* begins to explore the relationship of volumetric manipulations to the ground, it instigates further study on how the original operations can enhance or generate new ground conditions. Each design move has the potential to consider the ground. Steven Holl's *Correlational Programming*[1] diagrams inspire a unique understanding of four ground conditions: on the ground, in the ground, below the ground, and above the ground. *Conditional Design* will elaborate on several of these conditions through iterative operations.

The basic planar elements of stairs, apertures, and the abstracted ground are not to be interpreted as absolute or literal in their representation. Rather, the aim of introducing these spatial elements is to highlight the conditional opportunities yielded by the original operative moves.

[1]
Steven Holl. 'Correlational Programming' in *Parallax*. Princeton. New York 2000.

Combinations + Aggregations

With the foundation that verbs can be combined or one could operate multiple times using the same verb to develop several conditions, the combinations herein will focus on the highlighted conditions of aperture, connection, and the ground. There could be more than one occurrence of the operation in a given set of volumes, one operation could be used to explore multiple conditions, or one could explore distinct conditions through different operations. By using multiple design moves under the onus of a single operation, design consistency is established, especially when conditions are considered. For example, several **shifts** could produce multiple openings, or one could use the operation to create both openings and connections. By combining multiple operations, one could also expand on this consistency and develop a design hierarchy.

Once a condition is determined, the base volumes can be aggregated to study the multiplication of the condition. Any of the base aggregation operations - **array, stack, pack, reflect, join** - can be used to explore the potential of the series of conditions. For example, a connection is formed at the moment when multiple volumes **overlap**, so one could vertically aggregate the module by stacking the overlapping volumes while connecting each level of the massing.

Implementations

The operative approach provided not only a working method based on formal iteration, but also an opportunity to interpret existing built work. By further exploring volumetric manipulation at the scale of architecture, the conditional is present where formal moves are complemented by elements such as a connection between volumes or an opportunity for opening. The manner in which these volumes relate to the ground also refines these spatial ideas and moves them toward creating architecture.

When considering the assembly of multiple programmatic volumes, conditional moves can also begin to organize program. The connective element might delineate an area of utility versus a space of dwelling. Recall Pezo von Ellrichshausen's Poli House from *Operative Design*. The **offset** volume creates a perimeter thickened with program and utility. Through this operation of **offset**, Pezo von Ellrichshausen develops an overall volumetric manipulation, as well as local conditions within this larger move. Another project, the Wolf House, is a clear example of an **expanded** volume that is systematically formed while maintaining a clear organization of program. Along with the stairs, the operation creates a zone for service-based program (i.e. bathroom, utility, and mechanical spaces), while also defining dwelling spaces (living areas, bedrooms). This clear organization is clarified through the design move, or operation, **expand**. Pezo von Ellrichshausen handles these simple volumetric manipulations effectively, creating opportunities for circulation, a logic for openings, and careful consideration of the site. Solo House explores a clear design strategy through **lift** when circulation is created through this volumetric operation, in addition to highlighting how the original volumes relate to the ground.

These projects serve as strong examples of clear design logic, functional groupings of program, clean details, and overall consistency. As the program requirements, site, and general scale becomes specific to each project, the consideration of conditions becomes more significant.

Conditional Design can thus be useful as an interpretive device. Interpreting the implementations through the lens of *Conditional Design* allows one to appreciate the careful handling of spatial connections, openings, and site considerations unique to each project.

Solo House
Operation - Lift
Condition - Ground + Connect

Poli House
Operation - Offset
Condition - Connect + Open

Photos by Cristóbal Palma

Base Volumes + Elements

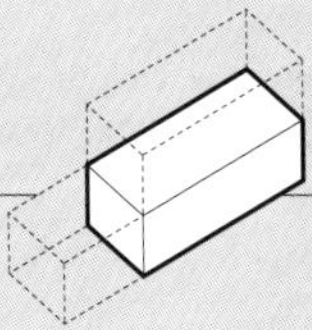

Variations on Base Volumes

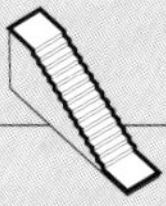

Element - Connection

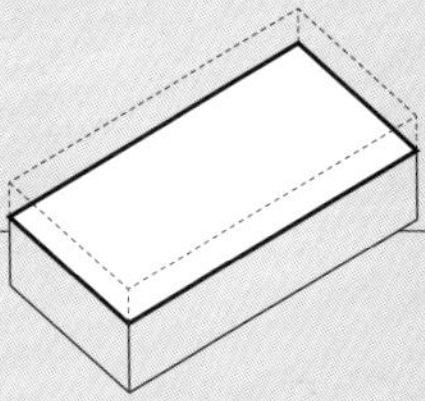

Element - Ground

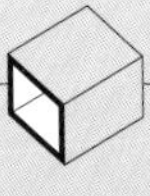

Element - Opening

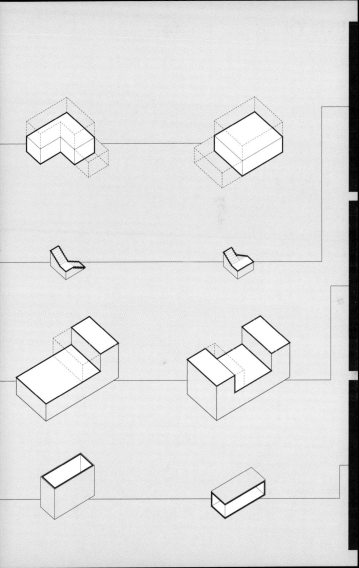

| 16 | Conditions |

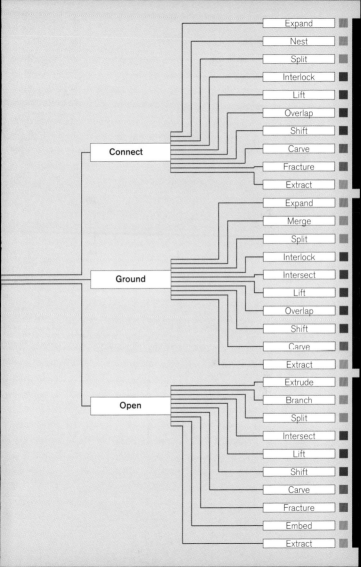

18   Conditions

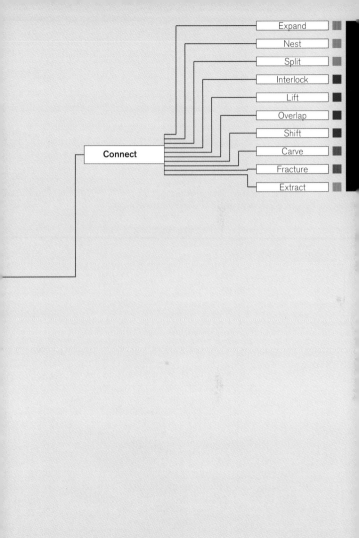

Connect

Expand
Nest
Split
Interlock
Lift
Overlap
Shift
Carve
Fracture
Extract

Expand

Condition | Connect

Operation - Expand

Condition - Connect

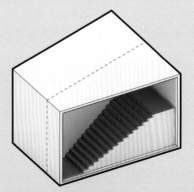

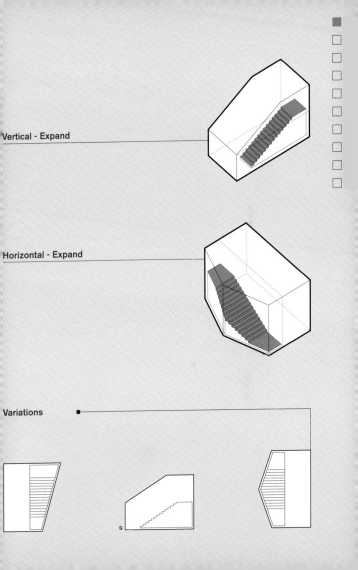

Vertical - Expand

Horizontal - Expand

Variations

Nest

Condition | Connect

Operation - Nest

Condition - Connect

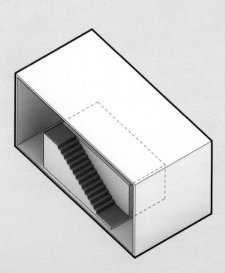

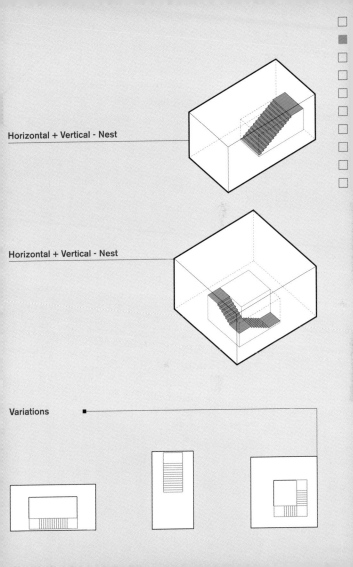

Horizontal + Vertical - Nest

Horizontal + Vertical - Nest

Variations

Split

Condition | Connect

Operation - Split

Condition - Connect

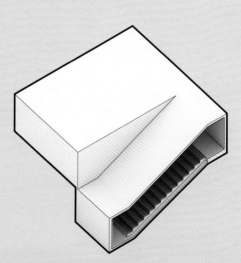

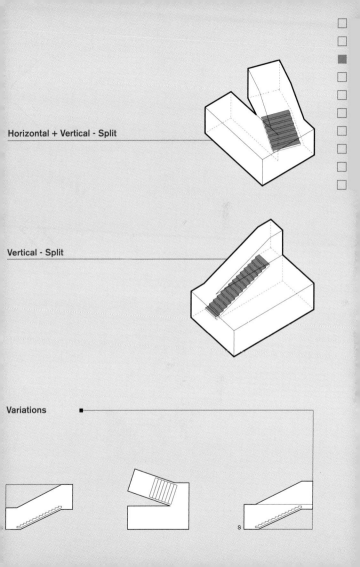

Horizontal + Vertical - Split

Vertical - Split

Variations

Interlock

Condition | Connect

Operation - Interlock

Condition - Connect

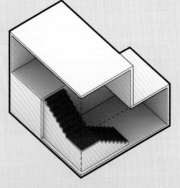

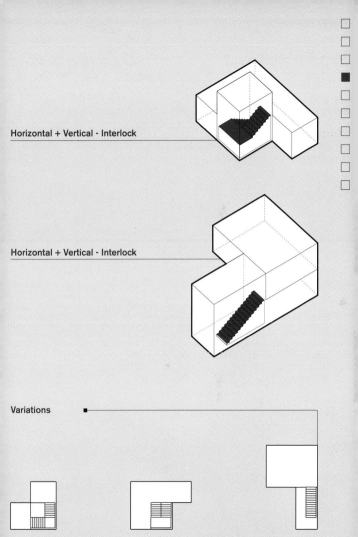

Horizontal + Vertical - Interlock

Horizontal + Vertical - Interlock

Variations

Lift

Condition | Connect

Operation - Lift _____

Condition - Connect _____

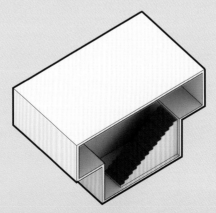

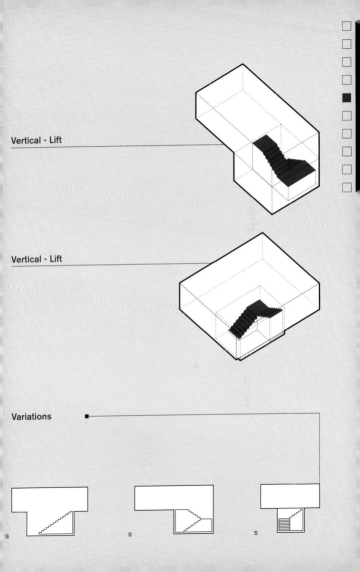

Vertical - Lift

Vertical - Lift

Variations

S S S

Overlap

Condition | Connect

Operation - Overlap

Condition - Connect

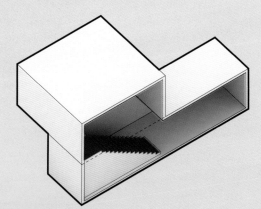

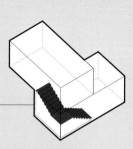

Horizontal + Vertical - Overlap

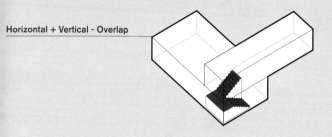

Horizontal + Vertical - Overlap

Variations

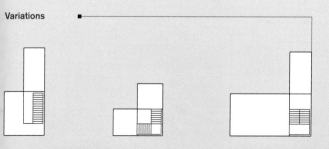

Shift

Condition | Connect

Operation - Shift

Condition - Connect

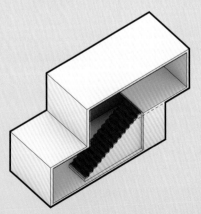

Vertical - Shift

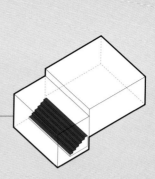

Horizontal + Vertical - Shift

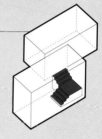

Variations

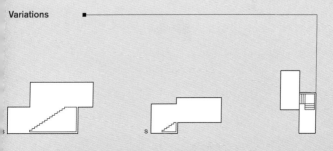

Carve

Condition | Connect

Operation - Carve

Condition - Connect

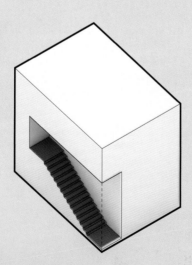

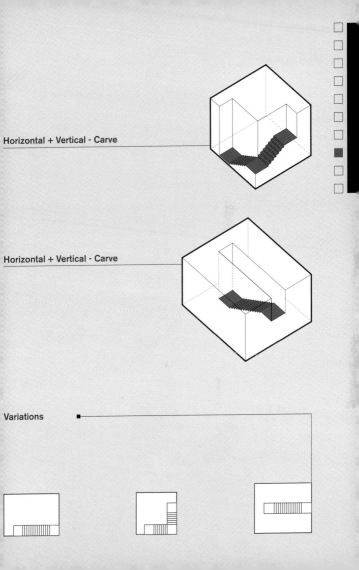

Horizontal + Vertical - Carve

Horizontal + Vertical - Carve

Variations

Fracture

Condition | Connect

Operation - Fracture

Condition - Connect

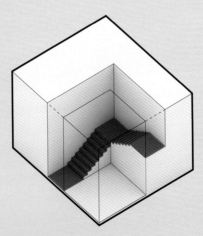

Horizontal - Fracture

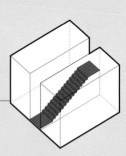

Vertical - Fracture

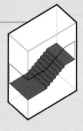

Variations

S

Extract

Condition | Connect

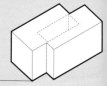

Operation - Extract

Condition - Connect

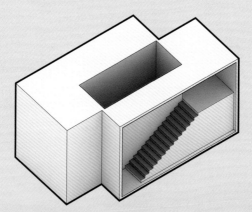

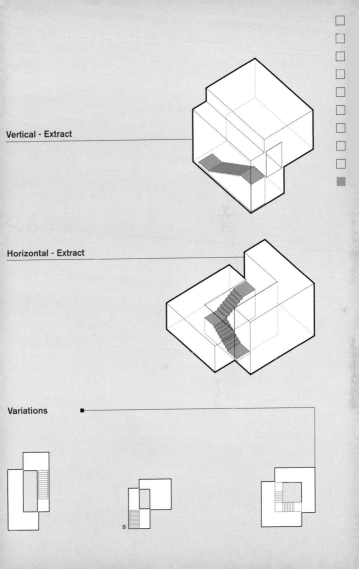

Vertical - Extract

Horizontal - Extract

Variations

S

Conditions

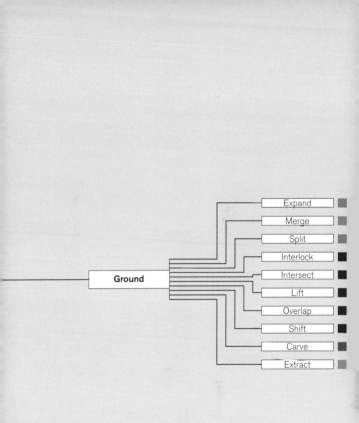

Ground

- Expand
- Merge
- Split
- Interlock
- Intersect
- Lift
- Overlap
- Shift
- Carve
- Extract

Expand

Condition | Ground

Operation - Expand

Condition - Ground

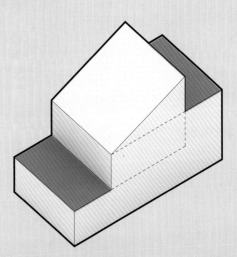

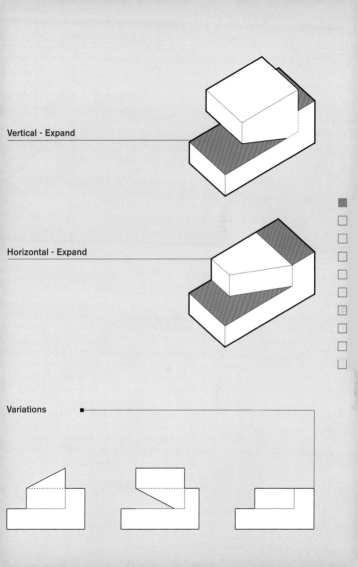

Vertical - Expand

Horizontal - Expand

Variations

Merge

Condition | Ground

Operation - Merge

Condition - Ground

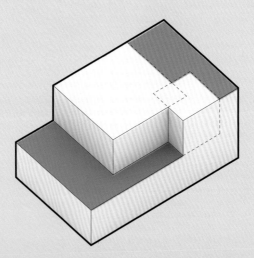

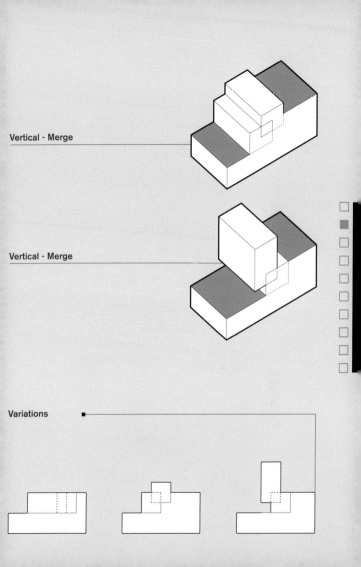

Vertical - Merge

Vertical - Merge

Variations

Split

Condition | Ground

Operation - Split

Condition - Ground

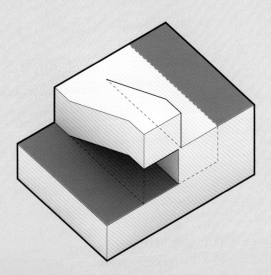

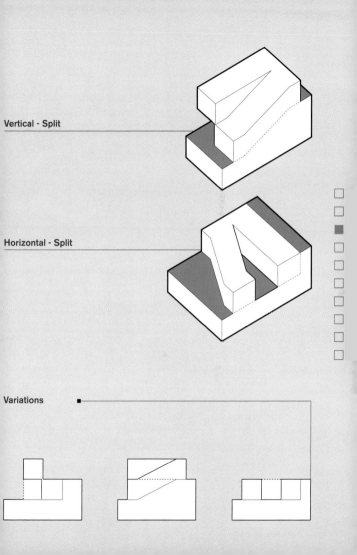

Vertical - Split

Horizontal - Split

Variations

Interlock

Condition | Ground

Operation - Interlock

Condition - Ground

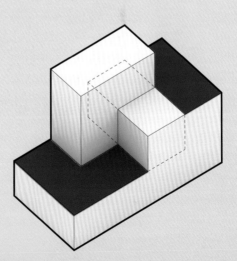

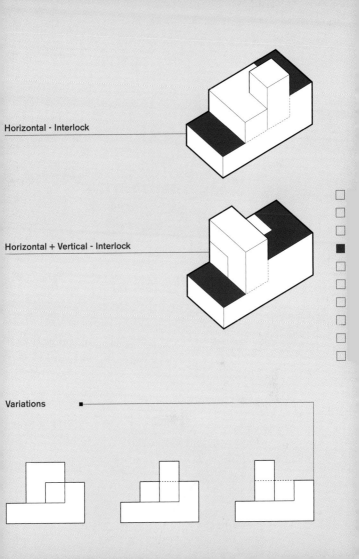

Horizontal - Interlock

Horizontal + Vertical - Interlock

Variations

Intersect

Condition | Ground

Operation - Intersect

Condition - Ground

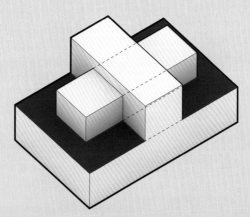

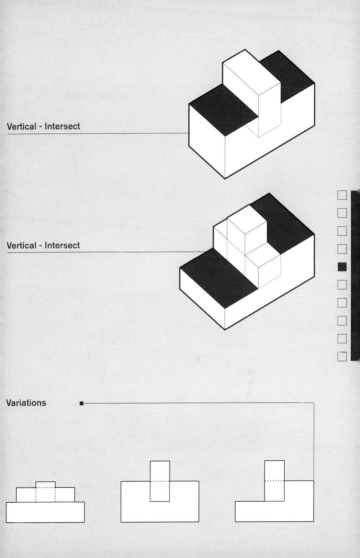

Vertical - Intersect

Vertical - Intersect

Variations

Lift

Condition | Ground

Operation - Lift

Condition - Ground

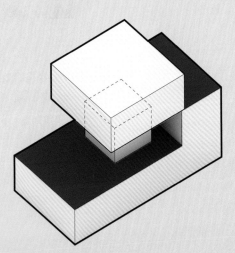

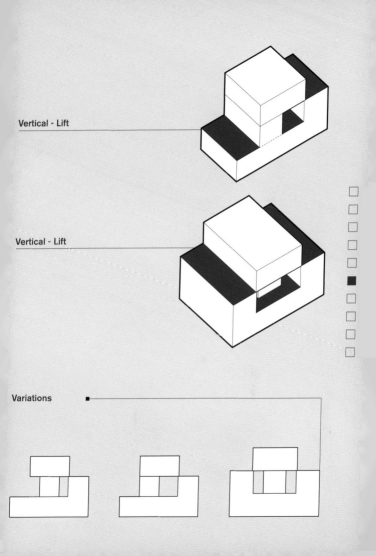

Vertical - Lift

Vertical - Lift

Variations

Overlap

Condition | Ground

Operation - Overlap

Condition - Ground

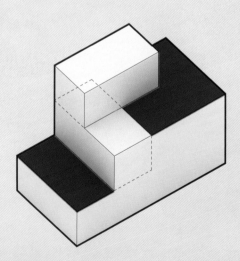

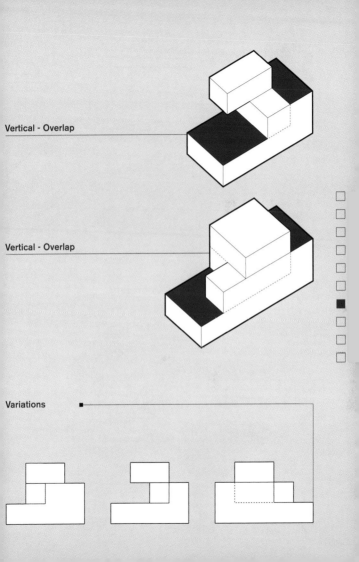

Vertical - Overlap

Vertical - Overlap

Variations

Shift

Condition | Ground

Operation - Shift

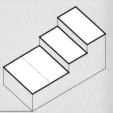

Condition - Ground

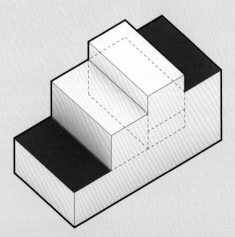

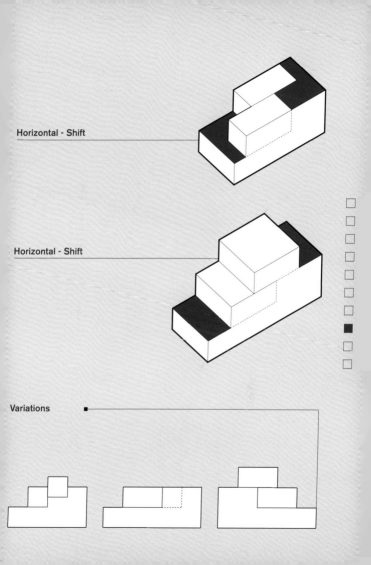

Horizontal - Shift

Horizontal - Shift

Variations

Carve

Condition | Ground

Operation - Carve

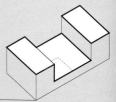

Condition - Ground

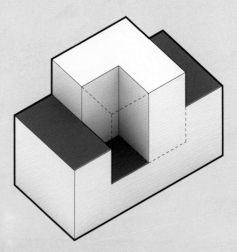

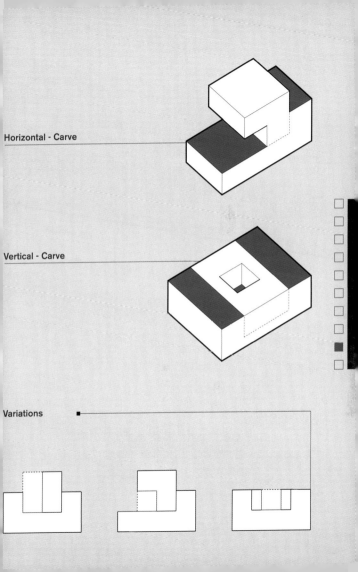

Horizontal - Carve

Vertical - Carve

Variations

Extract

Condition | Ground

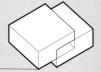

Operation - Extract

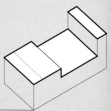

Condition - Ground

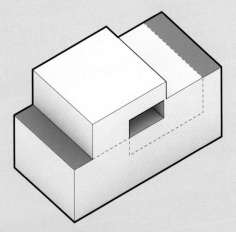

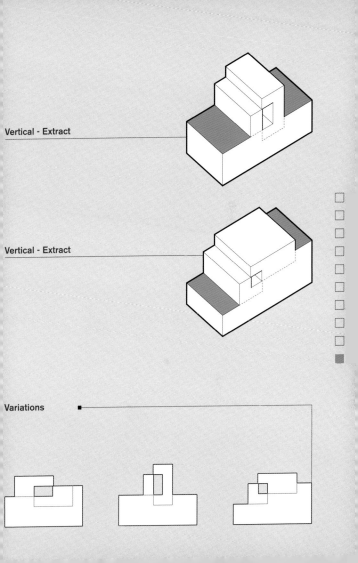

Vertical - Extract

Vertical - Extract

Variations

62 Conditions

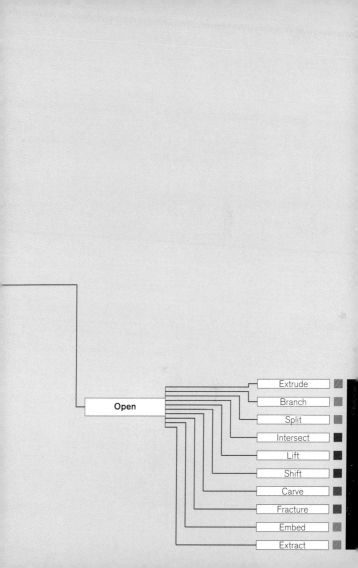

Open

Extrude

Branch

Split

Intersect

Lift

Shift

Carve

Fracture

Embed

Extract

Extrude

Condition | Open

Operation - Extrude

Condition - Open

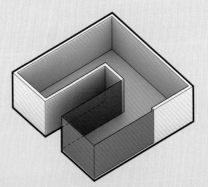

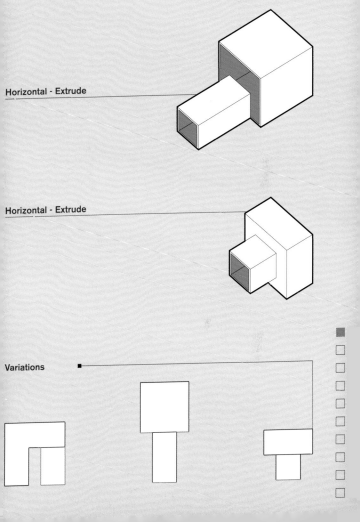

Horizontal - Extrude

Horizontal - Extrude

Variations

Branch

Condition | Open

Operation - Branch

Condition - Open

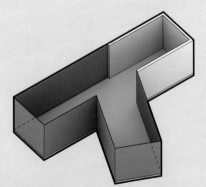

Horizontal - Branch

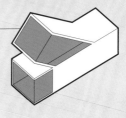

Horizontal + Vertical - Branch

Variations

Split

Condition | Open

Operation - Split

Condition - Open

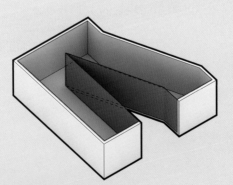

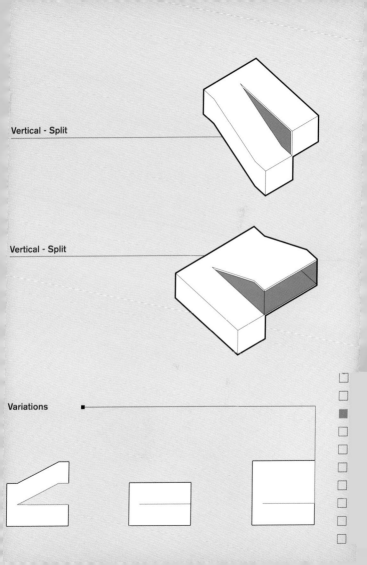

Vertical - Split

Vertical - Split

Variations

Intersect

Condition | Open

Operation - Intersect

Condition - Open

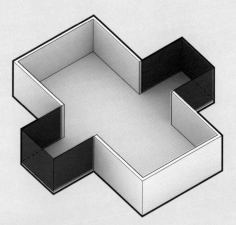

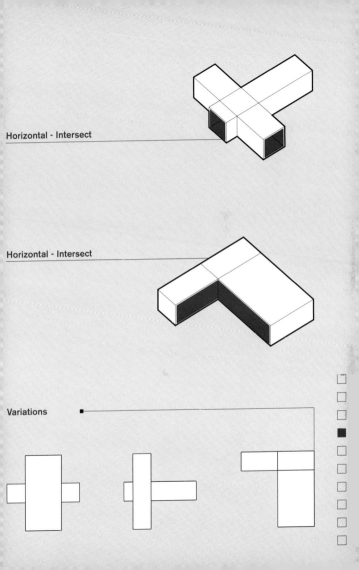

Horizontal - Intersect

Horizontal - Intersect

Variations

Lift

Condition | Open

Operation - Lift

Condition - Open

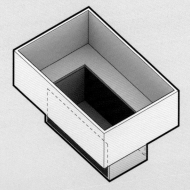

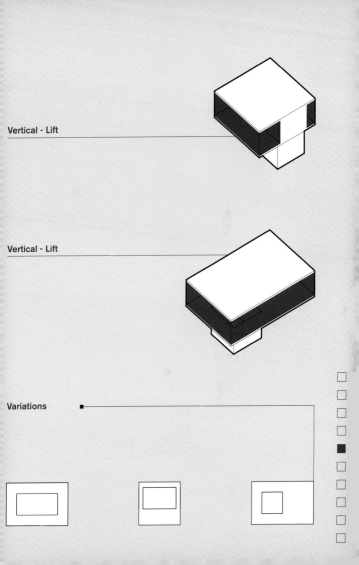

Vertical - Lift

Vertical - Lift

Variations

Shift

Condition | Open

Operation - Shift

Condition - Open

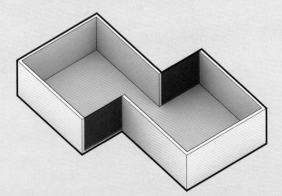

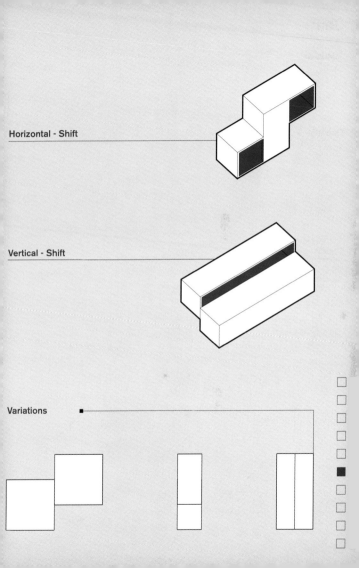

Horizontal - Shift

Vertical - Shift

Variations

Carve

Condition | Open

Operation - Carve

Condition - Open

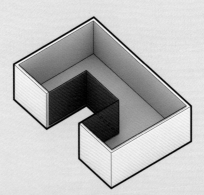

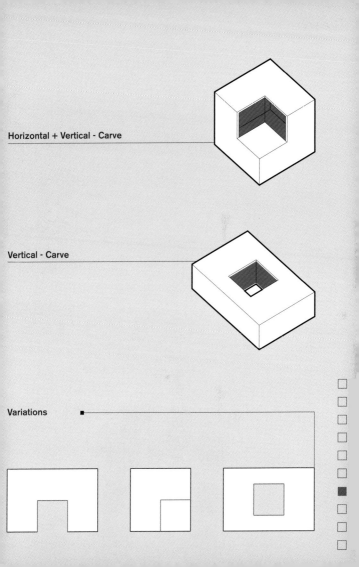

Horizontal + Vertical - Carve

Vertical - Carve

Variations

Fracture

Condition | Open

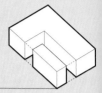

Operation - Fracture

Condition - Open

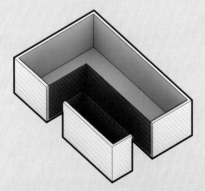

Vertical - Fracture

Vertical - Fracture

Variations

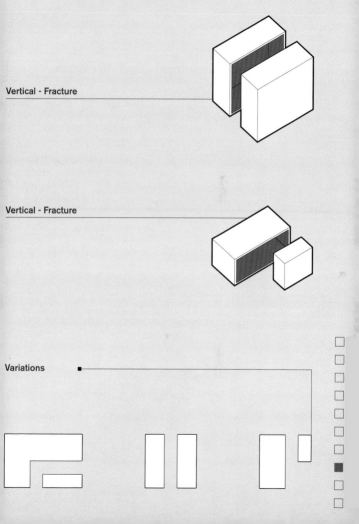

Embed

Condition | Open

Operation - Embed

Condition - Open

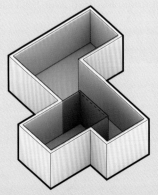

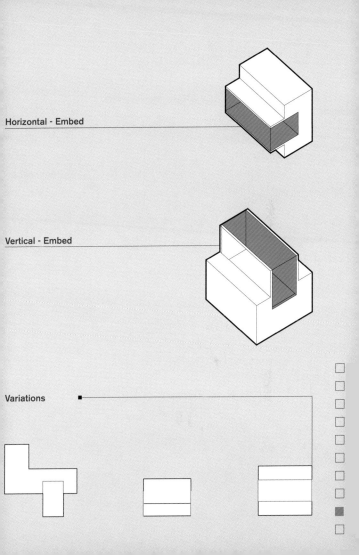

Horizontal - Embed

Vertical - Embed

Variations

Extract

Condition | Open

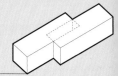

Operation - Extract

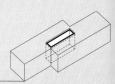

Condition - Open

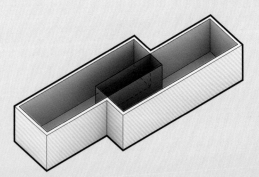

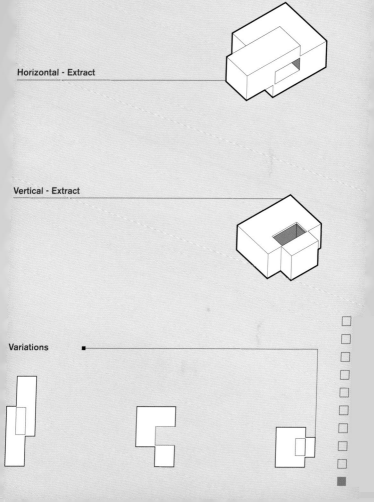

Horizontal - Extract

Vertical - Extract

Variations

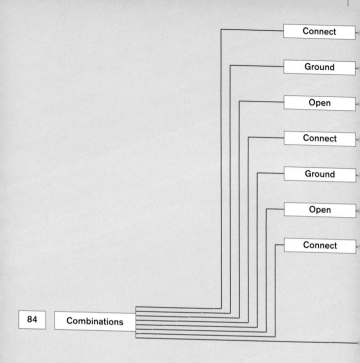

84	Combinations

Connect

Ground

Open

Connect

Ground

Open

Connect

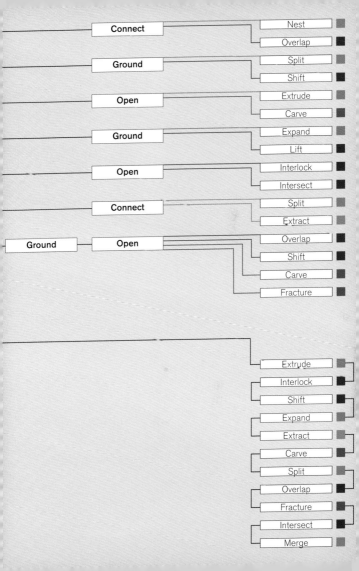

Connect
 ┌ Nest
 └ Overlap

Ground
 ┌ Split
 └ Shift

Open
 ┌ Extrude
 └ Carve

Ground
 ┌ Expand
 └ Lift

Open
 ┌ Interlock
 └ Intersect

Connect
 ┌ Split
 └ Extract

Ground — Open
 ┌ Overlap
 ├ Shift
 ├ Carve
 └ Fracture

Extrude
Interlock
Shift
Expand
Extract
Carve
Split
Overlap
Fracture
Intersect
Merge

Nest

Single Operation | Single Condition

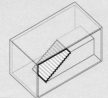

Condition - Connect

Condition - Connect

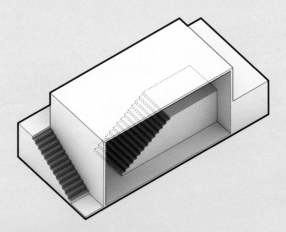

Overlap

Single Operation | Single Condition

Condition - Connect

Condition - Connect

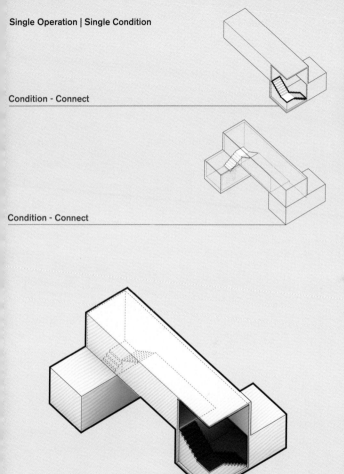

Split

Single Operation | Single Condition

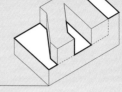

Condition - Ground

Condition - Ground

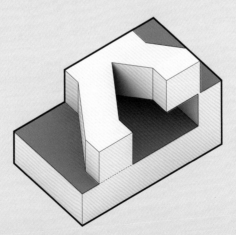

Shift

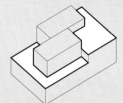

Condition - Ground

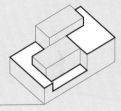

Condition - Ground

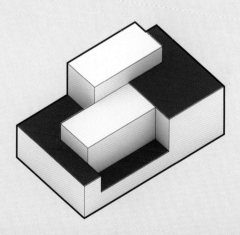

Extrude

Single Operation | Single Condition

Condition - Open

Condition - Open

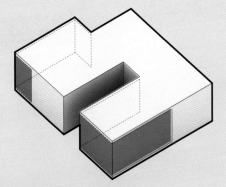

Carve

Single Operation | Single Condition

Condition - Open

Condition - Open

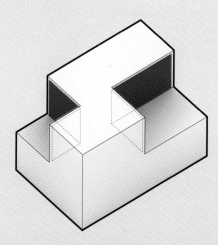

Expand

Single Operation | Multiple Conditions

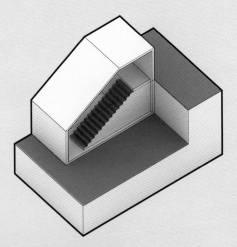

Condition - Connect

Condition - Ground

Lift

Single Operation | Multiple Conditions

Condition - Connect

Condition - Ground

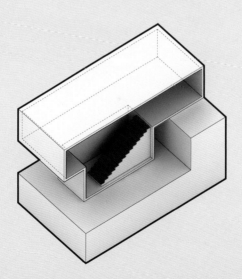

Interlock

Single Operation | Multiple Conditions

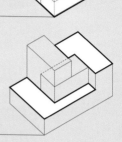

Condition - Open

Condition - Ground

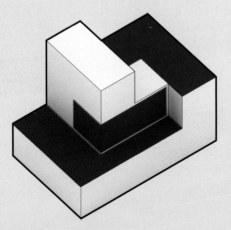

Intersect

Single Operation | Multiple Conditions

Condition - Open

Condition - Ground

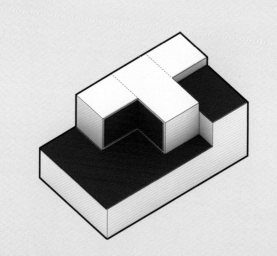

Split

Single Operation | Multiple Conditions

Condition - Open

Condition - Connect

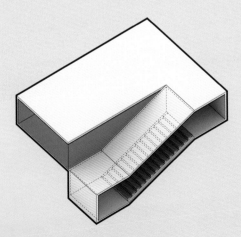

Extract

Single Operation | Multiple Conditions

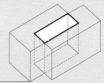

Condition - Open

Condition - Connect

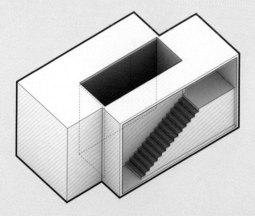

Overlap

Single Operation | Multiple Conditions

Condition - Open

Condition - Connect

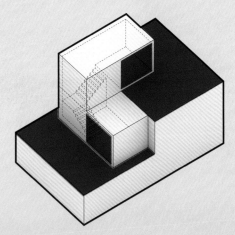

Shift

Single Operation | Multiple Conditions

Condition - Open

Condition - Connect

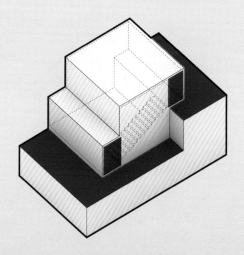

Carve

Single Operation | Multiple Conditions

Condition - Open

Condition - Connect

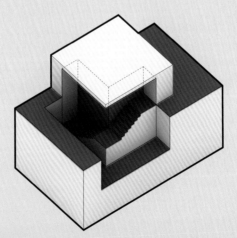

Fracture

Single Operation | Multiple Conditions

Condition - Open

Condition - Connect

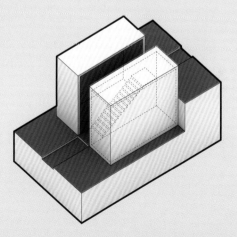

Interlock + Extrude

Multiple Operations | Multiple Conditions

Operation - Interlock | Condition - Connect

Operation - Extrude | Condition - Open

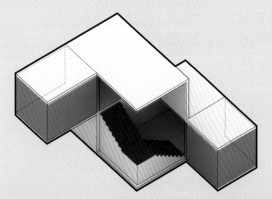

Interlock + Shift

Multiple Operations | Multiple Conditions

Operation - Shift | Condition - Connect

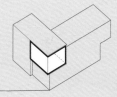

Operation - Interlock | Condition - Open

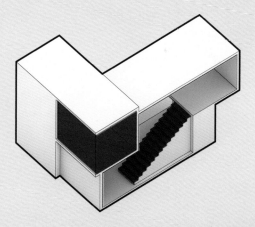

Shift + Expand

Multiple Operations | Multiple Conditions

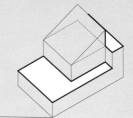

Operation - Expand | Condition - Ground

Operation - Shift | Condition - Open

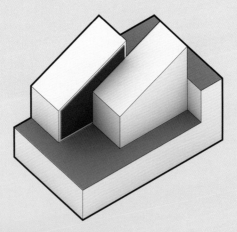

Expand + Extract

Multiple Operations | Multiple Conditions

Operation - Expand | Condition - Connect

Operation - Extract | Condition - Open

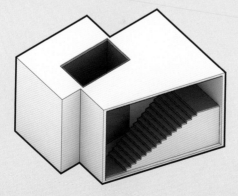

Extract + Carve

Multiple Operations | Multiple Conditions

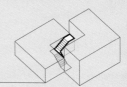

Operation - Extract | Condition - Connect

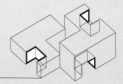

Operation - Carve | Condition - Open

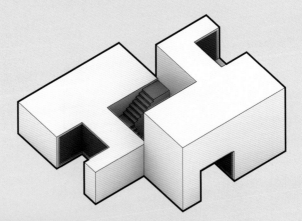

Carve + Split

Multiple Operations | Multiple Conditions

Operation - Split | Condition - Connect

Operation - Carve | Condition - Ground

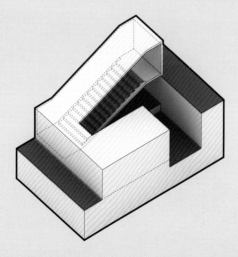

Split + Overlap

Multiple Operations | Multiple Conditions

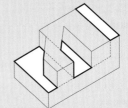

Operation - Split | Condition - Ground

Operation - Overlap | Condition - Connect

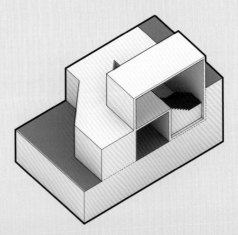

Overlap + Fracture

Multiple Operations | Multiple Conditions

Operation - Fracture | Condition - Connect

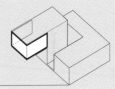

Operation - Overlap | Condition - Open

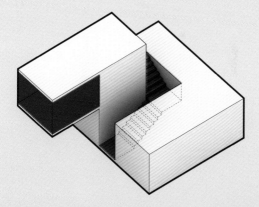

Fracture + Intersect

Multiple Operations | Multiple Conditions

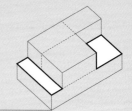

Operation - Intersect | Condition - Ground

Operation - Fracture | Condition - Open

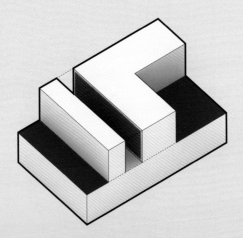

Intersect + Merge

Multiple Operations | Multiple Conditions

Operation - Intersect | Condition - Open

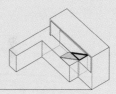

Operation - Merge | Condition - Connect

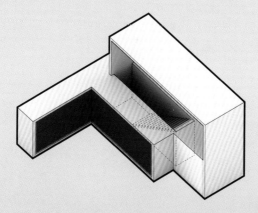

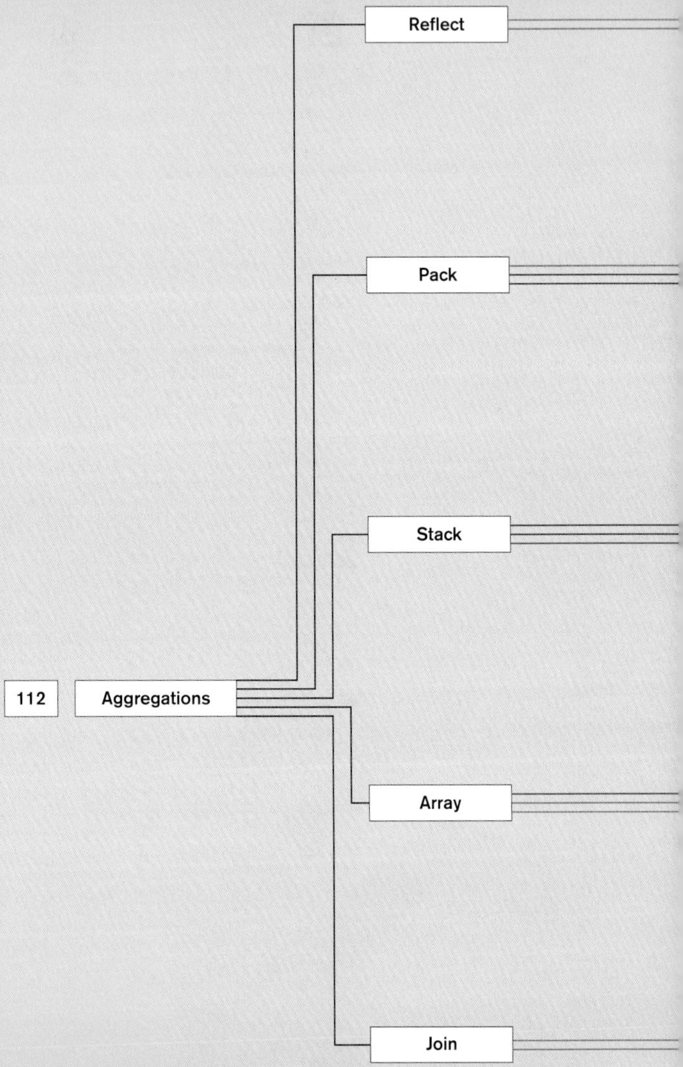

Reflect

Pack

Stack

112 Aggregations

Array

Join

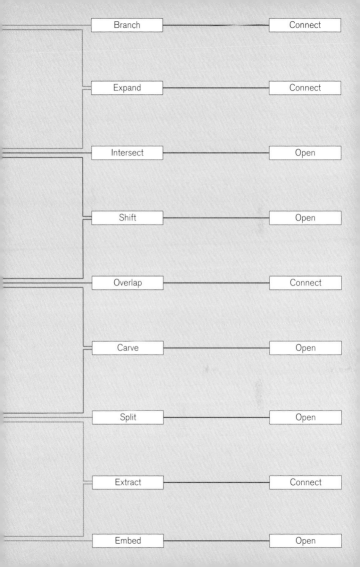

Reflect | Branch

Single Aggregation Method

Operation - Branch

Condition - Connect

Aggregation Method - Reflect
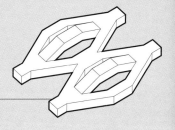

Condition - Connect
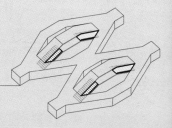

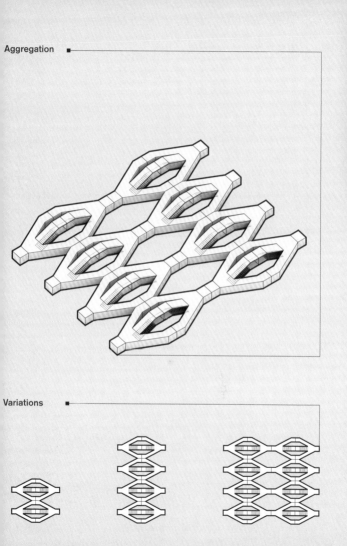

Aggregation

Variations

Reflect + Pack | Expand

Multiple Aggregation Method

Operation - Expand

Condition - Connect

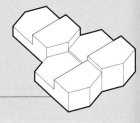

Aggregation Method - Reflect + Pack

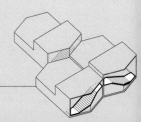

Condition - Connect

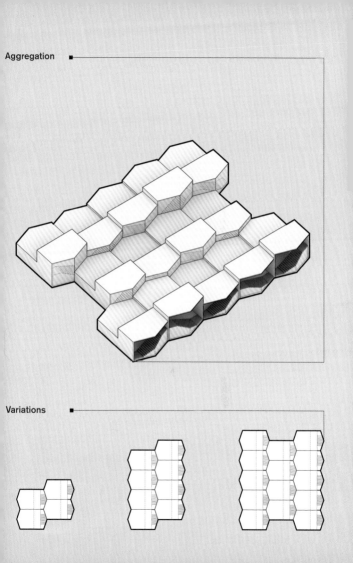

Aggregation

Variations

Pack | Intersect

Single Aggregation Method

Operation - Intersect

Condition - Open

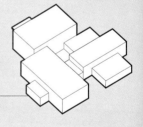

Aggregation Method - Pack

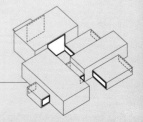

Condition - Open

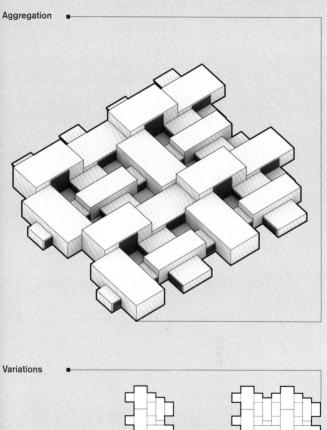

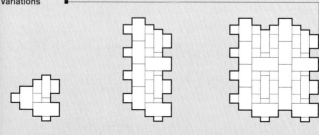

Pack + Stack | Shift

Multiple Aggregation Method

Operation - Shift

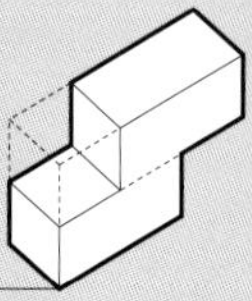

Condition - Open

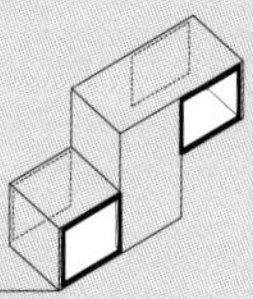

Aggregation Method - Pack + Stack

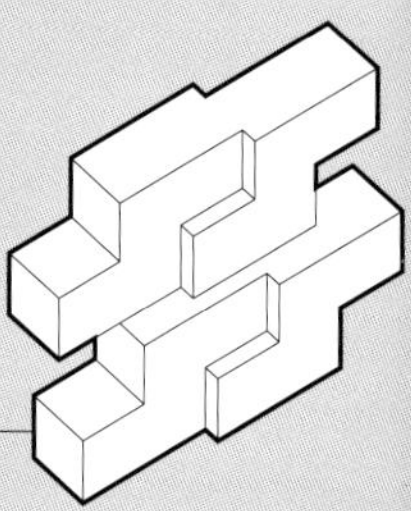

Condition - Open

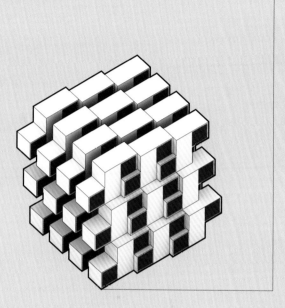

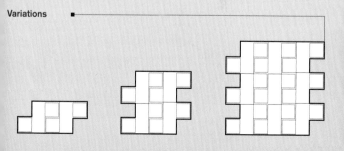

Stack | Overlap

Single Aggregation Method

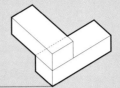

Operation - Overlap

Condition - Connect

Aggregation - Stack

Condition - Connect

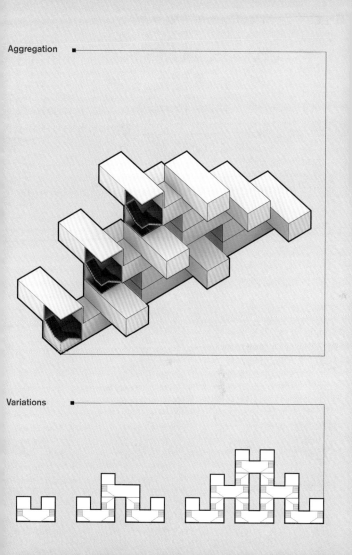

Array + Stack | Carve

Multiple Aggregation Method

Operation - Carve

Condition - Open

Aggregation Method - Array + Stack

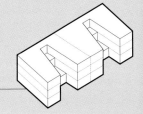

Condition - Open

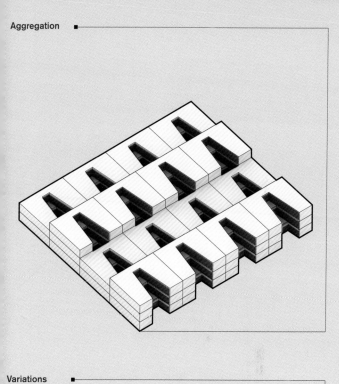

 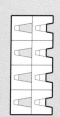 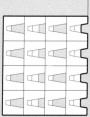

Array | Split

Single Aggregation Method

Operation - Split

Condition - Open

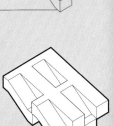

Aggregation Method - Array

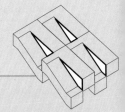

Condition - Open

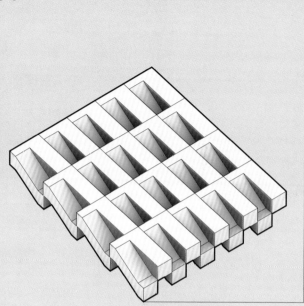

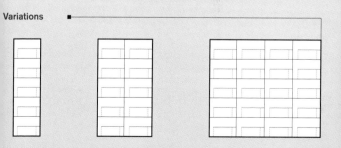

Join + Array | Extract

Multiple Aggregation Method

Operation - Extract

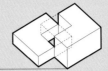

Condition - Connect

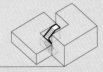

Aggregation Method - Join + Array

Condition - Connect

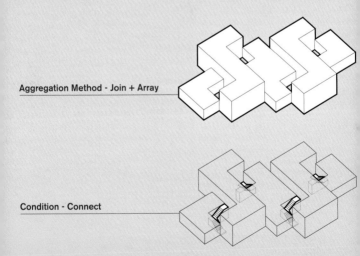

Join | Embed

Single Aggregation Method

Operation - Embed

Condition - Open

Aggregation Method - Join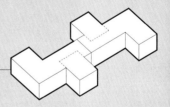

Condition - Open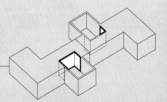

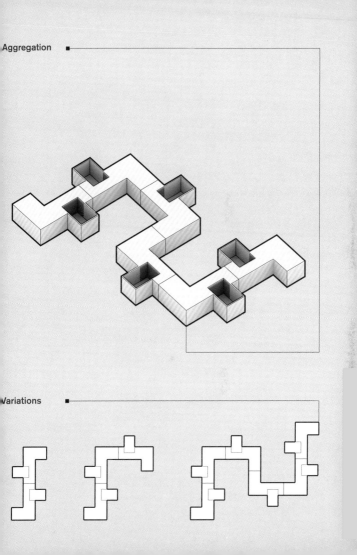

132 | Implementations

01 Arq - Lucernas House

Apollo Architects & Associates - Knot House

arnau estudi d'arquitectura - Bitten House

ARX Portugal + Stefano Riva - House In Juso

Colboc Franzen & Associés - House In Sèvres

Javier de Antón - Country House in Zamora

ODOS architects - Dwelling at Maytree

Oficina d'Arquitectura - House in Serra de Freita

Pezo von Ellrichshausen Arquitectos - Wolf House

Tetsushi Tominaga Architect & Associates - Gap House

Lucernas House

01 Arq

Photo by Aryeh Kornfeld

Embed

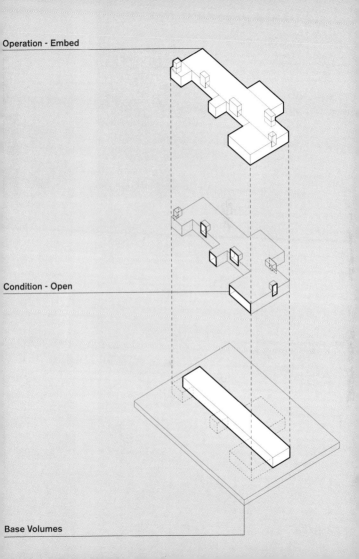

Operation - Embed

Condition - Open

Base Volumes

Knot House

Apollo Architects & Associates

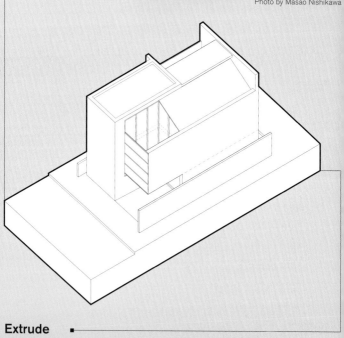

Extrude

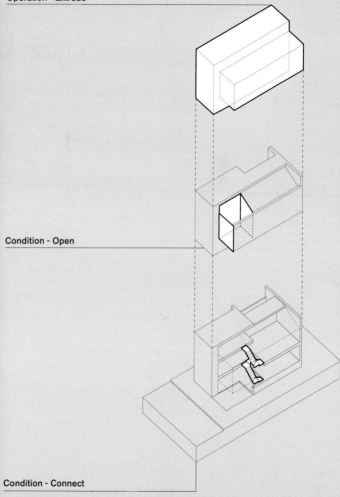

Operation - Extrude

Condition - Open

Condition - Connect

Bitten House

arnau estudi d'arquitectura

Photo by Marc Torra

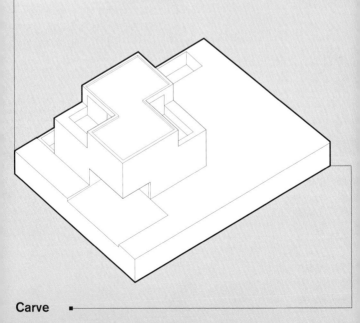

Carve

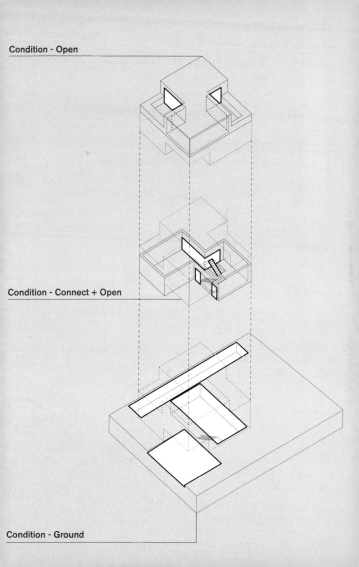

Condition - Open

Condition - Connect + Open

Condition - Ground

House In Juso

ARX Portugal + Stefano Riva

Photo by FG+SG fotografia de arquitectura

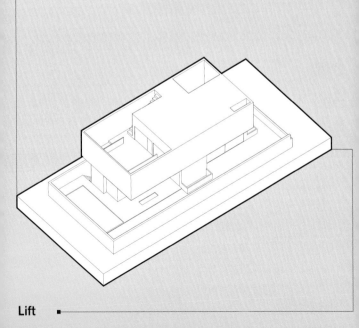

Lift

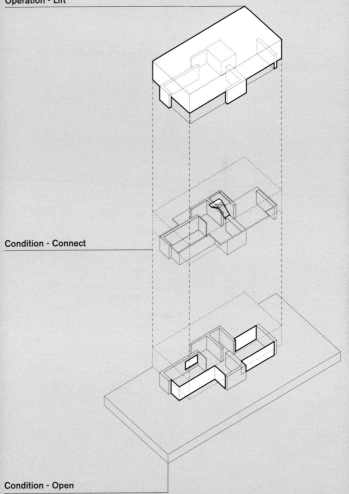

Operation - Lift

Condition - Connect

Condition - Open

House In Sèvres

Colboc Franzen & Associés

Photo by Cécile Septet

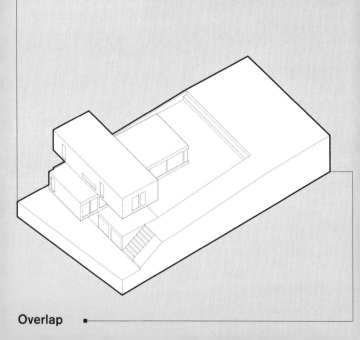

Overlap

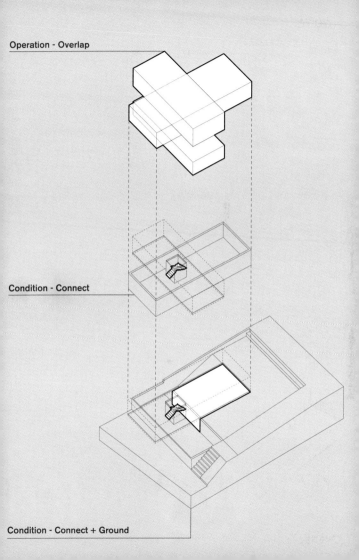

Operation - Overlap

Condition - Connect

Condition - Connect + Ground

Country House in Zamora

Javier de Antón

Photo by Esau Acosta

Intersect

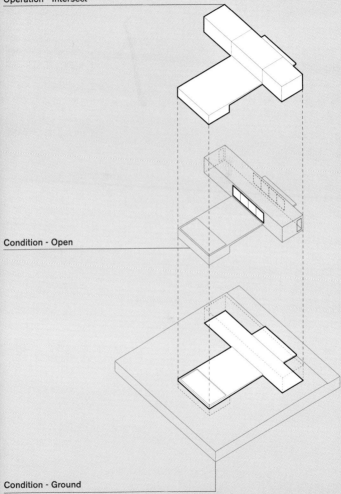

Operation - Intersect

Condition - Open

Condition - Ground

Dwelling at Maytree

ODOS architects

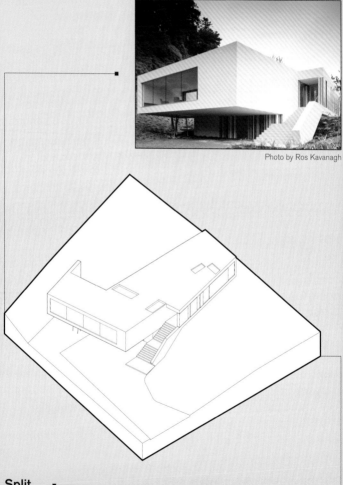

Photo by Ros Kavanagh

Split

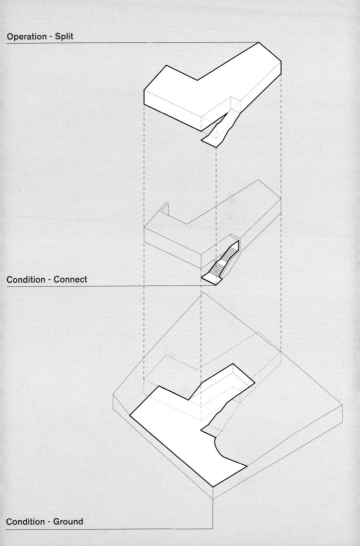

Operation - Split

Condition - Connect

Condition - Ground

House in Serra de Freita

Oficina d'Arquitectura

Photo by Oficina d'Arquitectura

Shift

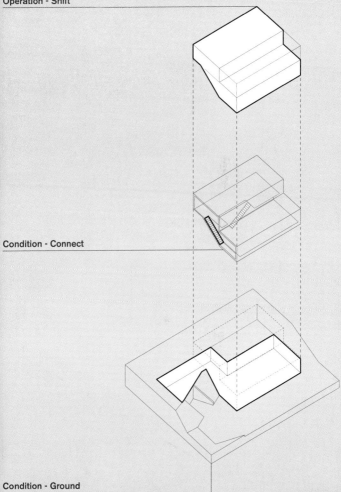

Operation - Shift

Condition - Connect

Condition - Ground

Wolf House

Pezo von Ellrichshausen Arquitectos

Photo by Cristóbal Palma

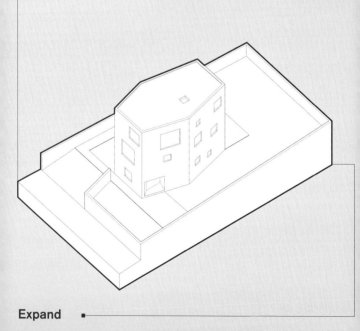

Expand

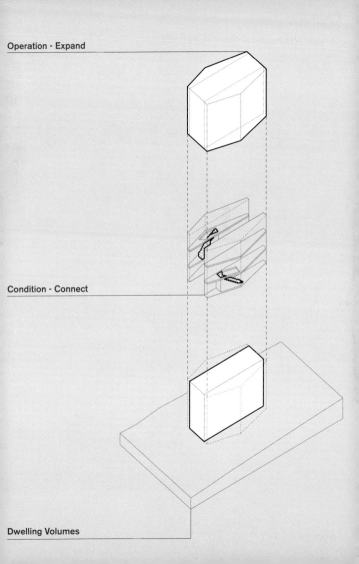

Operation - Expand

Condition - Connect

Dwelling Volumes

Gap House

Tetsushi Tominaga Architect & Associates

Photo by Suzuki Ken'ichi

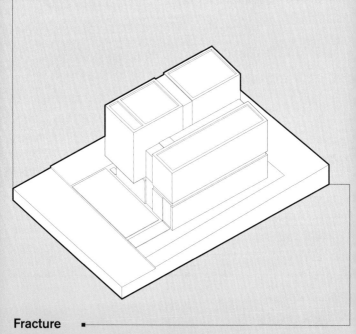

Fracture

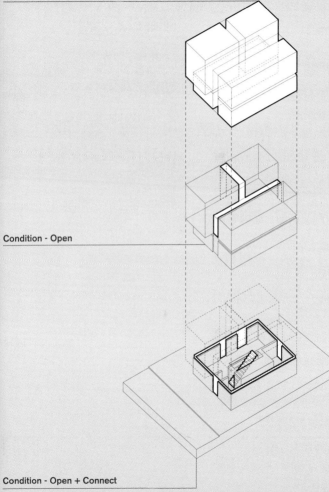

Operation - Fracture

Condition - Open

Condition - Open + Connect

Acknowledgements

To firms and photographers that have contributed to this publication :

01 Arq

Lucernas House
Photographer : Aryeh Kornfeld

Apollo Architects & Associates

Knot House
Photographer : Masao Nishikawa

arnau estudi d'arquitectura

Bitten House
Photographer : Marc Torra

ARX Portugal + Stefano Riva

House in Juso
Photographer : FG+SG fotografia
de arquitectura

Colboc Franzen & Associés

House in Sèvres
Photographer : Cécile Septet

Javier de Antón

Country House in Zamora
Photographer : Esau Acosta

ODOS architects

Dwelling at Maytree
Photographer : Ros Kavanagh

Oficina d'Arquitectura

House in Serra de Freita
Photographer : Oficina d'Arquitectura

Pezo von Ellrichshausen Arquitectos

Wolf House, Poli house, Solo House
Photographer : Cristóbal Palma

Tetsushi Tominaga Architect & Associates

Gap House
Photographer : Suzuki Ken'ichi

I am grateful

to the students with whom I have worked: the small group of architecture students from Tufts University and all my students from Northeastern University's School of Architecture. Our collaboration has inspired this book.

to BIS Publishers and to Rudolf van Wezel, for his consistent trust in my work.

to my friends and family, for their encouragement and pride in me.

to Sandra Roque, for her support and patience.

to Nora Yoo, for her continued help with this project, her editing, and advice.

Biography

Anthony Di Mari

Anthony Di Mari has taught fundamental architecture studio courses at Northeastern University's School of Architecture and Tufts University. He was a studio and drawing instructor at Harvard University's Career Discovery Program in architecture. He is the co-author of *Operative Design: A Catalogue of Spatial Verbs*. Anthony's current design research focuses on dynamic patterns, interactive fields, and land art.

www.anthonydimari.com